Barbara Sexton

the little book of
SMILES

Barbara
Sexton

the little book of
SMILES

Jo Mingles

ARCTURUS

PICTURE CREDITS – Ardea: 57 (John Daniels).
Corbis: 17 (Ole Graf), 18 (Patrick Ward), 20 (Sandra Seckinger), 21 (Jessica Peterson/Rubberball), 23 (Kelly Redinger/Design Pics), 26 (Kennan Ward), 29 (Ole Graf), 31 (Joe McDonald), 35 (Theo Allofs), 38 (Stephen Frink), 49 (Norbert Schaefer), 50 (Jason Stang), 51 (Winfried Wisniewski), 56 (Tamara Lackey), 58 (Stan Fellerman), 63 (Roger Ressmeyer), 79 (Tim Davis), 88 (Mike Kemp/Tetra Images), 92 (Jasper Cole/Blend Images), 93 (Darren Modricker). **Shutterstock:** cover, 6, 7, 8, 9, 10, 11, 12, 13, 14, 15, 16, 19, 22, 24, 25, 27, 30, 32, 34, 37, 39, 41, 42, 43, 45, 46, 47, 48, 52, 53, 55, 59, 61, 62, 64, 65, 66, 68, 69, 70, 71, 72, 73, 74, 75, 76, 77, 78, 80, 81, 82, 83, 84, 85, 86, 87, 89, 90, 91, 94, 95, 96. **Veer/Corbis:** 28 (pmphoto), 33 (Nikita Vishneveckiy), 36 (Yuri Arcurs), 40 (HamsterMan), 44 (Sergey Plakhotin), 54 (Adam Brill), 60 (Mikhail Dudarev), 67 (leaf).

ARCTURUS

This edition published in 2012 by Arcturus Publishing Limited
26/27 Bickels Yard, 151–153 Bermondsey Street,
London SE1 3HA

Copyright © 2012 Arcturus Publishing Limited

ISBN: 978-1-84858-185-2
AD002001EN

Printed in China

We love to see each other smile. And when we see a smile, it makes us smile, and smiles go on for miles and miles.

There are so many things that make us smile: joy, satisfaction, amusement, love, excitement and pleasure. Every smile reveals the feeling behind it and transmits a bit of that feeling to everyone who sees it.

'When you're smiling,' sang Louis Armstrong, 'the whole world smiles with you.'

Smiles light up the world.

And make everyone feel great.

We can smile at a private joke.

Or we may smile at someone else's expense.

Don't you just long to share the feeling?

Even the strongest among us can't control a smile.

Some smiles show you're eager to please.

Other smiles tell you who's boss.

Where is all this mouth coming from?

My goodness, I think I'm going to swallow myself!

We'll go to great lengths to give ourselves something
to smile about.

You have to work at it, you know.

We smile when we make a spectacle of ourselves.

Or something makes a spectacle of us.

Waiter, there's a fly on my nose!

**Don't you just love the smile that says,
'I know, I'm looking good?'**

Yep, I am the man.

I'm proud of my style, too.

It took me years to grow these beauties.

Well, you've got to smile to pull it off.

Some smiles are not to be trusted.

There are sinister smiles.

There are sadistic smiles.

There are guilty smiles.

And there are smiles of pure mischief.

There's no doubting the enthusiastic smile.

You can hear the eager brain cells spring into life.

You don't have to say anything, your face says it all!

Oh boy! There's no holding you back.

Hmm. Time to run, I think!

Just the promise of something good gets us smiling.

Did someone say fish?

Marvellous, you've come to look at my teeth!

Look, I've found a boat!

Would you like to hear my brilliant idea?

Some smiles are painted on.

Others say, 'It's OK, folks, I've done this before.'

The reassuring smile says, 'Stick with me, kid.'

Don't worry, I'm a professional.

I know things are going to turn out well.

First rule of performing – keep smiling!

If you want your audience to smile,

then show them the way.

Ta-dah!

And for our big finale...

Thank you very much, you've been a wonderful audience.

Hmm, there's more to smiling than just showing
your teeth, you know.

Anyone can see through a cheesy grin like that.

Who do you think you're kidding?

For real cheese, smile with your eyes.

The mouth says happy, the eyes say, 'What's for tea?'

We shouldn't have to force a smile, but sometimes we do.

Of course we're happy, aren't we, dear?

Happy? Me? Oh yes, of course!

Hurry up and take the picture, I can't hold this much longer.

Cheese!

Sadly, some of us find it hard to smile.

It's just a bit too much effort.

Even when we try, it doesn't quite fall into place.

You see, you have to be happy inside to make it work.

Maybe if you turn upside down and frown. How's that?

Sometimes we smile when we're not sure why.

We feel we want to smile, but there's
something that's not quite right.

There's a sense that something's about to go wrong.

Or perhaps it already has.

Hey! Where did all the snow go?

Courage is the ability to smile in adversity.

To put a brave face on a worrying situation.

Refusing to let the pain show.

Showing the world you will not be downhearted.

Even when you may be crying inside.

It's no use trying to cover up a smile.

It only makes the smile more obvious.

Are we trying to catch the smile for posterity?

Are we afraid that our eyes might pop out?

Why do we cover up the most attractive expression of all?

There's no holding back when you're feeling great.

The obvious delight when something you've hoped for
comes true.

When you embrace danger for the sheer buzz of it.

When you pull off an amazing stunt.

Or spend time with fantastic friends.

Then there's the smile of satisfaction at a job well done.

The blissful smile when we come to the end of a long, hard day.

Yes, that pleasing sense of accomplishment.

The happy feeling of enjoying your work.

The triumph when the whole thing turns out perfectly.

Friends who style together, smile together.

One smile usually leads to another.

How often do you smile like this on your own?

In fact, we tend to mimic each other's smile.

Because the thing we like most about our friends is their smile.

Barbara Sexton